GUERNICA — *1937*

THE SCULPTOR'S STUDIO *March 25, 1933*

SPRING ART BOOKS

KEITH SUTTON

SPRING BOOKS • LONDON

ACKNOWLEDGMENTS

The publishers wish to thank the following museums, galleries and collectors for their kind permission to reproduce the paintings in this volume: The Dowager Lady Aberconway (Plate I); Art Institute, Chicago (Plate III); Pushkin Museum, Moscow (Plate IV); Dr Vincenc Kramář (Plates V, XIV, XVI, XVII); Metropolitan Museum of Art, New York (Plate VI); Philadelphia Museum of Art (Plate VII); Museum of Modern Art, New York (Plates VIII, XV, XXI, XXIV, XXV); Hermitage, Leningrad (Plates IX, X); Roland Penrose, Esq., London (Plates XII, XXXVII); The Trustees of the Tate Gallery (Plates XIII, XLIII); Musée Nationale d'Art Moderne, Paris (Plates XIX, XXIX, XXXI, XLI, XLII); National Museum, Stockholm (Plate XX); Guggenheim Collection, New York (Plate XXVIII); Louis Leiris Gallery, Paris (Plate XXXVIII); Mrs Bertram Smith, New York (Plate XXXIX); Mr and Mrs Victor Ganz, New York (Plate XLIV); Mlle Angela Rosengart, Lucerne (Plate XLV). The paintings reproduced on Plates XXII, XXIII, XXVI, XXX, XXXII, XXXIII, XXXV, XXXVI, XLVI, XLVII are in the artist's collection. The paintings reproduced on Plates II, IV, VI, IX, X, XI, XV, XVIII, XIX, XX, XXI, XXII, XXIII, XXIV, XXV, XXVI, XXVII, XXVIII, XXIX, XXX, XXXI, XXXII, XXXIII, XXXIV, XXXV, XXXVI, XXXVIII, XLI, XLII, XLV, XLVI, XLVII, XLVIII were photographed by Photographie Giraudon, Paris. Hanover Gallery, London (Page 19, 20); Museum of Modern Art, New York (page 20 and Frontispiece); Artist's Collection. (Photographs supplied by Museum of Modern Art, New York) Page 19 and Frontispiece.

To T. E.

First published 1962
2nd impression 1963

Published by
SPRING BOOKS
WESTBOOK HOUSE · FULHAM BROADWAY · LONDON

Printed in Czechoslovakia
T 1299

CONTENTS

List of Black and White Illustrations

The signatures in the two black-and-white plates of 'The Sculptor's Studio' appear in reverse since Picasso signed the original plate which is always reversed in the course of printing.

INTRODUCTION

In trying to grasp what Picasso has meant to the art of this century, or to discover what most clearly characterises his work through a long and prodigiously productive life, one must first remember that he is more than a painter. He has produced masterpieces in sculpture and engraving, and has given fresh life and content to other media such as ceramics. At various periods of his development such activities have produced his most significant work.

Several of the other old masters of the Modern Movement exhibit a consistency of style throughout their lives that makes for an easier understanding of their art. With Picasso his very diversity of style masks his central character at the same time that it seems to reveal more facets of his personality. The extreme range of expression that he employs in his work, from lyrical classicism to a violent expressionism, presents problems of acceptance to those people who feel that the one must exclude the other. But extremes of passion are no more mutually exclusive in art than they are in personal relationships. To come to an understanding of Picasso's art one must think of him as a constructive rather than a destructive personality. Even in works that seem to shatter our illusions as to the harmony of the human body and spirit, such as *Guernica* (Frontispiece), or the *Woman dressing her hair*, 1940 (Plate XXXIX), he is asserting, by the very act of creating the image, that compassion is possible even at the instant of man's disillusionment. He gives to a painting like *Guernica* the coherence and the structure of a Greek pediment.

The first thing to recognise, in searching for a unity behind the diversity of his work, is that Picasso is an idealist. Allowing that the function of art is to transmute what in reality is almost unbearable, what in life is so moving because it is so beautiful or so frightening that we can hardly face it straight for ourselves, then the attitude of an artist who takes such experiences apart for us and puts them together again in a manner that we can look at them, is certainly idealistic. Picasso's action in creating a work of art is one of faith in man's ability to construct as well as to destroy. Normally we find such idealism is itself unbearable, otherwise we would not approve of it in others while mocking it in ourselves. In recognising the enormous demands it makes on any person, we may become jealous of an artist just because he can do something about it. But the artist's optimism is to be shared; all good work is a celebration of affection.

Picasso was born in Malaga, Spain, in 1881. His family had lived in the town for at least two generations. His father, Don José Ruiz Blasco, was an artist, a tall man with reddish hair and an elegant, slightly withdrawn and reticent manner that encouraged his friends to refer to him as 'the Englishman'. He lived amongst an active circle of artists, poets and musicians; even his landlord was a sympathetic patron of the arts who, on occasion, accepted pictures in lieu of the rent from hard-pressed tenants. Life was never too easy for the family however, and when Don José took on the responsibility for his unmarried sisters and his mother-in-law and when his son, Pablo, was born, he accepted a post in the School of Fine Arts and Crafts of San Telmo, as well as the curatorship of the local museum. The relationship between an artist son and an artist father must always be one of subtle psychological involvement that only the two persons concerned can evaluate. They may hold into later life incidents of an affecting nature that have perhaps been expressed in a single word or in an action, with no dramatic gesture to remember it by. The published remarks of Picasso concerning his father have always been of an affectionate kind. For his part, his father encouraged Pablo, and when the time came that he had to recognise the extraordinary nature of his son's talents, far outstripping his own and pointing in what must have seemed disquieting directions, he did nothing to retard him even if he could no longer persuade him. Picasso's mother, Maria Picasso Lopez, whose family name Picasso later took, was younger than her husband. She was a small and delicately made woman, with sparkling black eyes and a vivacious temperament, characteristics which she passed on to her son.

Though Picasso has spent less than half his life in Spain, he remains essentially attached to his home country and has never forgotten what he learnt from El Greco, Velasquez and Goya. Indeed he has continued all his life to re-assess his relation to the art of the past, as witness Plate XLV, the *Portrait of a painter, after El Greco* (1950), or the enormous sequence of paintings inspired by Velasquez's *Las Meninas* which Picasso produced in 1957.

In deliberating on what is particularly Spanish in Picasso's art one is guided more by the sensibilities and the general mood of a work rather than by specific details.

Plenty of things in his work make one think, 'this is his volatile nature taking over', 'this is the love and passion for extroverted drama of the Spanish people', 'this is the clear light of the Mediterranean sun' or 'this is the simple severity of Romanesque and Catalan art', and so on. Certainly there are the specific images of the bull-ring which take on ambivalent forms in many works: the Minotaur, the bull surveying the carnage of *Guernica*, or the broken and heroic horse in the same painting. But these images have either been given a wider context than their origins in real life, or they have themselves helped to create the image we have of Spain — rather than the other way round.

Equal in importance to dramatic events or environment, particularly for a young artist and one trying to establish himself in a foreign country as Picasso was in Paris in 1900, is remembrance of the family group and that strong sense of pride and loyalty which is characteristic of the Spanish nation. Such an artist, feeling his isolation, is likely to try and erect in his work images that are equivalent to the situations he is parted from, or images which express his sympathy with people who are in a like position. Thus, I feel that Picasso, very early in his career, turned to allegory as a means of expressing his own deepest emotions. (See notes on the *Family of Saltimbanques*, Plate III, and *The acrobat and the ball*, Plate IV).

But before then, Malaga, Madrid, and Barcelona provided a fertile environment for the young artist, who could indulge in youthful and heady romanticism as he began to measure himself up in the liberal society of the cafés.

At the turn of the century the northern area of Spain was more open to the liberalising influences of her French neighbour, and there was a constant exchange of intellectuals moving between Paris and Barcelona. Not all the aesthetic and political ideals came from France, however; Ibsen and Wagner were as attractive, and as seemingly easy to digest, as the more elegant culture of France. Certainly the expressionist content of more Northern art struck a responsive chord in a country whose primitive artists had combined in the Catalan frescoes the highly sophisticated formalities of the Byzantine style with simple but passionate outbursts of emotion.

Picasso formed friendships in these years that, with characteristic loyalty, he has carried through his life. But his instincts and his ability to absorb ideas led him to seek wider influences. In October 1900 he went to Paris for the first time. He returned home for the New Year but went back to Paris early in 1901. He was obviously impressionable and affected by the sheer verve and pace of what he found there. He engaged and disengaged, in his work, with the styles of Post-Impressionism like a dancer changing partners at the Moulin de la Galette. He had his first exhibition at the gallery of Vollard in June (see note, Plate 1), returning to Barcelona in December 1901. But between those first two visits to Paris a change of mood took place that was to colour his work for several years. The precise reasons for this change remain obscure but probably several factors had their effect; amongst them must have been Picasso's recognition that he must inevitably separate from the conventional respectability of his family in order to live and shape his own life. His adoption of his mother's family name 'Picasso' occurs at this time and may be seen, without too much stress, to indicate not only where his natural feelings lay, but also to discover what was unique and individual to himself, away from the traditional aspirations of his family.

Whatever the causes of the change, the term 'colour' can be used in a literal manner because the styles into which his work successively fell, or have since been divided, are generally known as Blue, Rose and Terra-cotta; not names that help to distinguish what is most important in each work or style, but accurate enough as labels in that each stresses a particular mood. The Blue period paintings are, in particular, obviously romantic expressions of emotion, and it is not surprising to find that Picasso should have looked towards the expressionist characteristics of an artist like Toulouse-Lautrec.

Though many of his pictures in the early years of this century involved poetic allegories that were generalised in their content — like *The old Jew* or *Life*, both of 1903 — Picasso's actual progress was away from the vaguenesses which surrounded the continued use of Impressionism and its techniques. His own work began to express a much greater sense of plasticity of form, the figures could be felt to be displacing air, not merely being bathed in light. By the time he finally moved to Paris in 1904, his melancholy had lifted a little and the spirited company of new-found friends and companions, particularly that of the beautiful Fernande Olivier, gave him a sense of self-confidence, though it never eliminated his inner conflict and self-criticism.

His confidence was to be tested in the next few years: for although Picasso's quality as an artist was quickly recognised, by advanced dealers and critics as well as by friends, when the really dramatic advances of Cubism were made, in the years 1907 onwards, even his closest acquaintances were shocked at first. In spite of his self-containment as an artist, able to work as he needed in isolation, he, like all artists, must have hoped for a perceptive response from those who might have understood him best.

Picasso has joked with the public, verbally rather than pictorially, but the humour, or irony, that is evident in his art is there because, for Picasso, life is not whole without humour as well as tragedy. When he jokes or prods people into a reaction it is in order for them to see more clearly and feel more deeply, but he is aware that an immediate reaction may not be one of affection. From those who should know better he expects more. When they disappoint him, his distress is the greater. Except in rare and valuable instances of personal relationship, the loneliness of the artist is a full-time occupation.

A prelude to the outcries that were to arise with the advent of Cubism is illustrated by *Portrait of Gertrude Stein*, 1906 (Plate VI), with its postscripted remark by the artist against those who voiced outraged feelings and claimed a lack of facsimile in the painting: 'never mind, in the end she will manage to look just like it.' The sitter obliged; keeping the portrait by her until her death. In the end, when we have seen and come to understand a Picasso picture, we begin to search nature for the truths that we have missed, as already we look out of our windows at the trees that the Impressionists have created for us, or we look round at our breakfast-table and recognise how like a Bonnard it is.

In spite of his concern with landscape and still life, it is the human body and its features to which Picasso has given most intense expression in his art. He causes us to regard the figure in a new light, he forces us to trace back to our own experience things that we have often felt but not expressed; or he shows us something that we may have noted in a casual way, but not, for ourselves, considered as the subject-matter of art: such things, for example, as the pyramid-shaped feet of peasants or fishermen, that recur in his work, things that we may have seen as often as the artist. The actual deformity of the feet springs from their function in hard, daily life. Picasso gives them a dignity that is beautiful when understood; they have exchanged the grace of athleticism for the power of a significant occupation.

Picasso notices such things more frequently than most people, he perceives their significance and gives them expression. He is, indeed, one of the most empathetic of men. He is able to feel into the nature of a physical stress in a body as deeply as he feels the emotional content of the figures in his paintings. It has been noted that Picasso's own physique is small but compact and well-built, and that his hands are of great shapeliness. He has always shown a corresponding regard for the size and well-developed bodies of athletes; perhaps it is an instinctive compensation that informs the proportions of his youths on beaches (*Pipes of Pan*, page 19) or the drawings of dancers at the bar, and gives them a Roman cast, so that their agility is combined with power. His own hands were a feature that he continued to draw and model long after he had given up making self-portraits.

But it is the human head that has fascinated him most, holding for him more wonder and mystery, demanding more re-appraisal, than any other feature. Picasso did not paint his own head again after the *Self-portrait* of 1906, though he makes reference to himself either in allegorical disguise or in an occasional profile attached to a painting (see note, Plate VII).

The *Self-portrait* (Plate VII), and the ***Seated nude*** (Plate V) of the same year, illustrate clearly the direction in which Picasso was moving. It may be easy now to appreciate their simplicity and solidity of form, but at the time it must have been a shock for his friends, who valued the charm of his earlier work. It placed Picasso in an even more isolated position because, in his determination to achieve a vitality through aesthetic discipline, he was running counter to the interests and enthusiasms of those progressive artists whom he most admired. Matisse, Braque and Derain were involved in the style that became known as Fauvism in which almost all the weight of form and content was given to colour. But Picasso wished to create a tangible, three-dimensional quality in his painting, and he had become impressed and influenced by Cézanne's search for a geometric basis to his composition, the much-quoted search for the forms of cylinder, sphere and cone that underlie nature. Cézanne tried to paint things as if he held them in his hand; Picasso seems actually to inhabit the object of his attention. He even gets into the 'sensations' of objects not normally regarded, by visual appearances, as being animate; he can bring to life a coffee-pot or a vase and imbue it with comic-erotic intentions towards other objects on the table (Plate XXXII).

In the winter of 1906—7 Picasso set about what was to be his largest and most important work to date, *Les Demoiselles d'Avignon* (96 × 92 in.). For it he made numerous studies and afterwards he made many pictures that were, in effect, postscripts. The picture itself (Plate VIII), is more a gathering together of his potential than a summary of his past achievement. Picasso did not see the change that this picture adumbrates as being a complete renunciation of his former work. To him it was a development, but one that demanded temporarily renouncing certain hard-won successes in order to make a necessary progression. The achievement, in artistic terms, was supported by a victory in personal terms.

By the end of 1906, Picasso, at the age of twenty-five, had already gained an enviable reputation and a status amongst the most perceptive circles in Paris. This position had itself been gained without compromising his painting, although it was not accompanied by much greater financial affluence, and he had gone through real hardship in recent years. Now, not only was his work being collected by such discerning people as the Steins, but he had shown to the art world his mastery of diverse media: painting, sculpture, drawing and engraving. His future was regarded as even more brilliant by persons of sympathy and artistic authority. It would not have been unreasonable to find him following the line of his successes, now that so much resistance had been overcome. Picasso's stock-taking was not, however, concerned with consolidation. It took great courage to turn his back on what he was most admired for.

He had always been prone to conflicting doubts, even when the feeling in his work appeared most secure and generous. His personal conflict increased rather than diminished with the repose and contentment he had found when working in Gosol in the summer of 1906. (See note to Plate V.) As so often in his career, two contrasting tendencies in style were concerning him at the same time. On the one hand there was an open, decorative and ebullient form of design, and on the other, the calm and severe simplifications of the recent nudes. These latter attempted to realise, to the utmost degree, the volumes of the forms depicted. Added to this immediate conflict were the accumulated impressions and half-absorbed influences of style, some foreign and exotic, others primitive, with which Picasso had been charging his mind since he had begun painting. This is evident, in one instance, in the apparently arbitrary manner in which the two startling heads on the right of *Demoiselles* are left in cursory, but adequate, attachment to the bodies. Their Negroid influence is hardly integrated into the composition; they were perhaps added shortly after Picasso first showed the picture to his friends, but they heighten rather than disrupt the gradual change of style from left to right across the picture. In spite of these heads with their 'barbaric' accents of colour, the colour is restricted to pinks and blues, and the forms have become clearly defined and static. It is the first real link to be hammered out between African and Western art, and the works that followed in the years 1907—9 less violently mark the transition of style that is known as the Negro period, although, because what came out of that period was more significant than the individual influences that went into it, it would be more reasonable to call it Proto-Cubist.

The *Demoiselles* was not, of course, an achievement that could stand alone for long, although its impact on the world at large was long delayed by its remaining in the artist's studio for many years. Picasso worked in close association with Braque in the following years, and the interplay and sympathy of idea between them was such that distinguishing their work became, at one point, very difficult.

The two years following the *Demoiselles* were full of energetic research and experiment (Plates IX and X), not all of them successful in that many of the pictures remained unfinished, or at least were not carried through to a completely covered canvas. This is not in itself a sign of lack of conviction in a work, for Cézanne had already asserted pictorial situations of the same kind where a picture showed more concern with the process by which it was being painted than concern for achieving a methodical and even finish. But by late 1909 Picasso had distilled a method, rather than a style, of painting, whereby he could match his impulses and imagination with a technique that was at once assured and speculative. He could enquire into the nature of reality and speak of his discoveries in a consistent language. This crystallisation, in both senses of the word, began the period now known as Analytical Cubism which lasted between late 1909 and 1912 (Plates XI to XVI).

Like most terms connected with art, 'Analytical' refers to the spirit rather than to the letter of its meaning. Neither Picasso or Braque, although they were aware of the analogies with geometry and space-time physics, ever pretended that their researches and analyses were mathematical or scientific. It was sensibility that counted. It was the critics of Cubism who in time became concerned with theory.

Nevertheless both artists clarified and systematised what they felt to be a new conception of an artist's experience. The path Cubism took involved great discipline of mind and emotion. The intention behind a Cubist picture is a desire by the artist to understand form and to bring together those aspects of a particular object or figure that most completely and convincingly realise its character. The artist wishes to prove the existence of the object rather than to suggest its appearance by illusionistic methods. This means showing several aspects of the object, external and internal, that could not possibly be seen from one view. But as such aspects are necessary to tell us what is happening under the surface or behind the object, the artist presents us with a 'simultaneity' of viewpoints. To do this on a flat, two-dimensional surface of a canvas means abandoning such conventions of illusion as central perspective. It also means inventing or creating new harmonious conjunctions of form that do more than one job at a time.

That is why certain features in a Cubist picture, once we have decided on their identity, seem to slip from our grasp the harder we stare at them; once recognised, they begin to assert another function in the picture. This may be structural or compositional rather than descriptive. Notice, in the *Portrait of Uhde* (Plate XII), how the plane that defines his left shoulder can first be read as his shoulder; then as a plane connecting with his right shoulder and thus marking the angle of his chest to the front of the picture; and then again the same plane appears to come forward until it is almost the nearest thing to us, and then it begins to look like a piece of paper that the sitter might well be reading as he sits so still.

The method of working in any case requires a close co-ordination of figure and its background, so that in spite of the light and atmosphere that is to be found in the picture, the formal effect of the space is like that of a low-relief sculpture. It enhances the roundness of a form that sharply curls away from the background — such as in the passage around the neck of Uhde. The touching and overlapping of the many little facets and planes builds up over the picture, and extends the sense of structure. In later works, those of 1911 and 1912, this more even spreading-out of the structure over the surface accentuates and stresses that flatness of the picture plane, and reminds us once again of the sophistication of the whole aesthetic process. This phase, known sometimes as Hermetic Cubism, moved more and more towards abstraction, and the element of detachment on the part of the artist increased until, at one point, the pictures were left unsigned to stress the distancing of personal emotion.

But Picasso's pictorial intelligence was always backed by an instinctive passion and a reliance upon sensibility and impulse. This he could not suppress. As the followers of the movement began to codify the system into rigidity and geometrical theory, Picasso began to put the cat back into the bag.

The re-appearance of a literal and impudent reality began with the re-introduction into the picture of arbitrary, though not arbitrarily placed, colour accents, and by the use of lettering on the picture surface as part of the composition. This lettering had an allusive function (Plates XV and XVI), a connection with everyday existence. Soon both Picasso and Braque extended this representation of the 'unsterilised' and tactile world to the point where they actually incorporated pieces of material on the canvas surface itself (Plate XVII). *Collage*, simply a word arising from the French *coller*, 'to stick together', led in its turn to Picasso working in low relief with various materials and occasionally making assemblage sculpture. These latter pieces were often made in an unstable material and with an almost deliberate casualness of construction, which meant that they did not all survive for long. One can speculate how far this indifference to permanence, in a medium traditionally associated with just that quality, was due to an instinctive reaction to the serious and monumental aims of Analytical Cubism. Certainly the phase that began with *collage* in 1912, known as Synthetic Cubism, shows an all-round lightening of attitude and a general embracing of the more sensuous visual pleasures of life and art (Plates XVI to XIX). Certainly, also, a great deal of what had gone on in progressive art between 1905 and the beginning of the First World War was intended to disrupt conventional values and habits of seeing and thinking about art. What is so remarkable, at this distance of time, is that so many of the bombs that went off under outmoded traditions caused such beautiful explosions and left us with so many fine works of art.

It would have seemed that, even for Picasso, Cubism could not go beyond this realisation of 'temporary' sculpture. But he took the opportunity actually to set it in motion and saw it come alive when he designed the costumes and scenery for the ballet *Parade* in 1917 (see note to Plate XXI). That particular interlude in Italy not only helped to lighten the glooms of the war, but put Picasso back in contact with the theatre world, a world where dedication and personal imaginative authority go hand in hand; a world peopled by exotic, extravagant, but highly sensitive, personalities. Perhaps too, it was the intimations of death that surround a war that led him once again to characterise and delineate the features of his friends: this time in a highly refined but flexible style of drawing that recalls the neo-classicism of Ingres. Renewed contact with the Mediterranean also influenced the mood of classical antiquity that recurs in the paintings of this period and the next few years (Plates XXIII and XXIV).

Picasso was roundly denounced by some of his erstwhile followers for betraying Cubism and returning to a realism they could not accept. But Picasso had never thought of Cubism as an end in itself. When it began to look as though that was what it was becoming, he was the first to shift his ground. Nor was it true in fact that he had abandoned the method, for not only did he summarise the attainments of Synthetic Cubism in the two great paintings of 1921, both called the *Three musicians* (Plate XXV), but he continues to use the Cubist idiom today with all the self-possession of a man who knows, so to speak, how to sharpen a pencil properly.

Surrealism is a style that draws its power from the juxtaposition of two or more images that are not normally thought of in relation to one another; real and suggested things are brought together as in a dream and they move or disturb us by their effect on our irrational and emotional responses. Thus one should speak of one Surrealist work at a time because, although all such works rely upon general subconscious experiences, each work of art is unique.

The first significant work of Picasso that could be called Surrealist is a remarkable painting of 1913, usually known as *Woman in a chemise*. This painting was later shown with acclaim by the Surrealists in their London exhibition of 1937. While Picasso did not follow this particular work by a series in the same style, there is always an element of Surrealism in the *collages* that he produced at about the same time.

The real eruption of sardonic Surrealism occurs with *The three dancers* of 1925 (Plate XXX), a picture that grimly mocks the image of a bacchanal with intimations of mortality, as if it were more a 'Dance of Death'. The golden aftermath of optimism that followed the First World War had faded for Picasso as it had done for others. Added to which, the pressure of his private emotional affairs led him to inhabit more constantly the underworld of his own brooding subconscious, like a distracted Orpheus seeking for all his Eurydices.

But not all the art that rises from such stimulus relies on a frenetic expression and a wild imagery; the pastoral and melancholy air is just as effective and expressive of emotional disturbance. Many of the figures in Picasso's pictures in the following years were cast into a day-dreaming trance (Plates XXXIV and XXXV). The swimming figure in the small *Women and children on the beach*, 1932 (Plate XXXIII), has exchanged her rational environment of water for the sky: she might be floating in either.

It is in the Surrealist, or partly Surrealist, works of Picasso that the disturbance to the familiar appearance of the human figure seems greatest. For some people such works go beyond what they can bear to face; for them, distortion is seen as deformity, as an assault motivated by hate on the part of the artist. In reality, I believe, such works by Picasso come closer to the possessive blindness of love; dramatised love maybe, but sincere and passionate in the extreme. The greatest example of such emotional anger, purified by the processes of art and thus made eloquent for other people, is *Guernica*.

This great mural, painted for the Spanish Pavilion in the Paris Exhibition of 1937, was certainly inspired by a personal anguish at the situation in his native country. Picasso's general thoughts about how to carry out his commission were activated by the specific incident of the destruction of the small Basque town, by German bombing planes flying for General Franco, on April 28th of that year. The picture was painted with great speed but with no signs of haste in the finished composition, only acute passion. On May 10th he began to paint the large canvas (11′5½″×25′5¾″), following a series of preliminary drawings and studies; in June the finished mural was installed. The composition had developed on the canvas as work proceeded, and radical alterations took place within the framework of Cubist simplicity. The colour is entirely black, white and grey, and yet so effective is it in establishing a horrifying reality that someone, recently recollecting the picture after a number of years, argued strongly that it did contain colour.

Picasso has given no detailed explanation of the iconography of the painting, but his preparatory drawings and the photographs that were taken during its execution are some help in tracing certain private images that had already been given allegorical allusion in his earlier works. Chief amongst these are the image of the dying horse that goes back to a drawing of 1917, and that, more recently, found expression in the dramatic *Bullfight* of 1934 (Collection Mr and Mrs V. Ganz). More personal is the ambivalent image of the bull, and the Minotaur, that makes equivocal appearances in the series of etchings known as *The sculptor's studio*, 1933, engaging in activities that vary between the affectionate and the ferocious. Finally both horse and Minotaur are joined by the figure of a young girl holding a light in the large etching called *Minotauromachia*, 1935. The image of the woman holding the light over the carnage of *Guernica* is the one image that remained constant, in its significance and its form, from the very first drawings to the finished painting.

Guernica is a deliberately public statement and it has clearly, over the years, succeeded in speaking directly to all kinds of people of the horror and futility of war, whatever side of an argument they were on. And yet it is expressed by images that are sometimes relatively obscure and are private to the artist. They are carried out in a visual language of forms having their origins in Cubism. *Guernica* typifies the power of an artist to make an impersonal statement about something that he feels most deeply. The distance and perspective that his aesthetic judgement gives to such a work enables it to retain its impact for every occasion on which we look at it. We can bring our own emotions to play amongst its tangled tragedy, but its own conviction and structure take us out of ourselves so that we can share the burden of our private anguish.

As was suggested at the beginning of this introduction, it has been necessary to focus on those periods of Picasso's career that were most formative and original in innovation for the artistic styles of this century. I have tried here, and in the following notes, to read the character of the man through his public works. Certain characteristics may, however, be usefully mentioned at this point.

Picasso is a typical 'nest-builder', that is, a man who takes over his immediate surroundings and clutters them up with his familiar objects and private possessions, or fills them soon enough with his own new productions. As an artist, he is at a practical disadvantage in relation to, say, a writer, who can carry the paraphernalia of his trade in his pocket. Then again, Picasso is sensitive to the nature and mood of his environment. He has remarked that he only seems to draw his fauns and other arcadian personalities when near the Mediterranean coast. So he will make an excursion to change his mood, as in the summer of 1908, when he went to the lush and heavy landscape of La Rue-des-Bois, north of Paris. Or he may be forced to evacuate, as to Royan during the last war (see note, Plate XI), but on the whole he has travelled on an axis through familiar territory, between Paris, the Mediterranean and Spain. His moves have been changes of situation rather than travels of exploration.

Given his initial graphic talent, he was able to put his hand on any idea that appealed to him, to hold it down and dissect it in an immediate and an intimate way. When he felt that an idea could not be expressed graphically on its proper scale, then he would reach out into whatever medium seemed necessary to exploit his discoveries, heedless of whether that medium had been used in such a manner before.

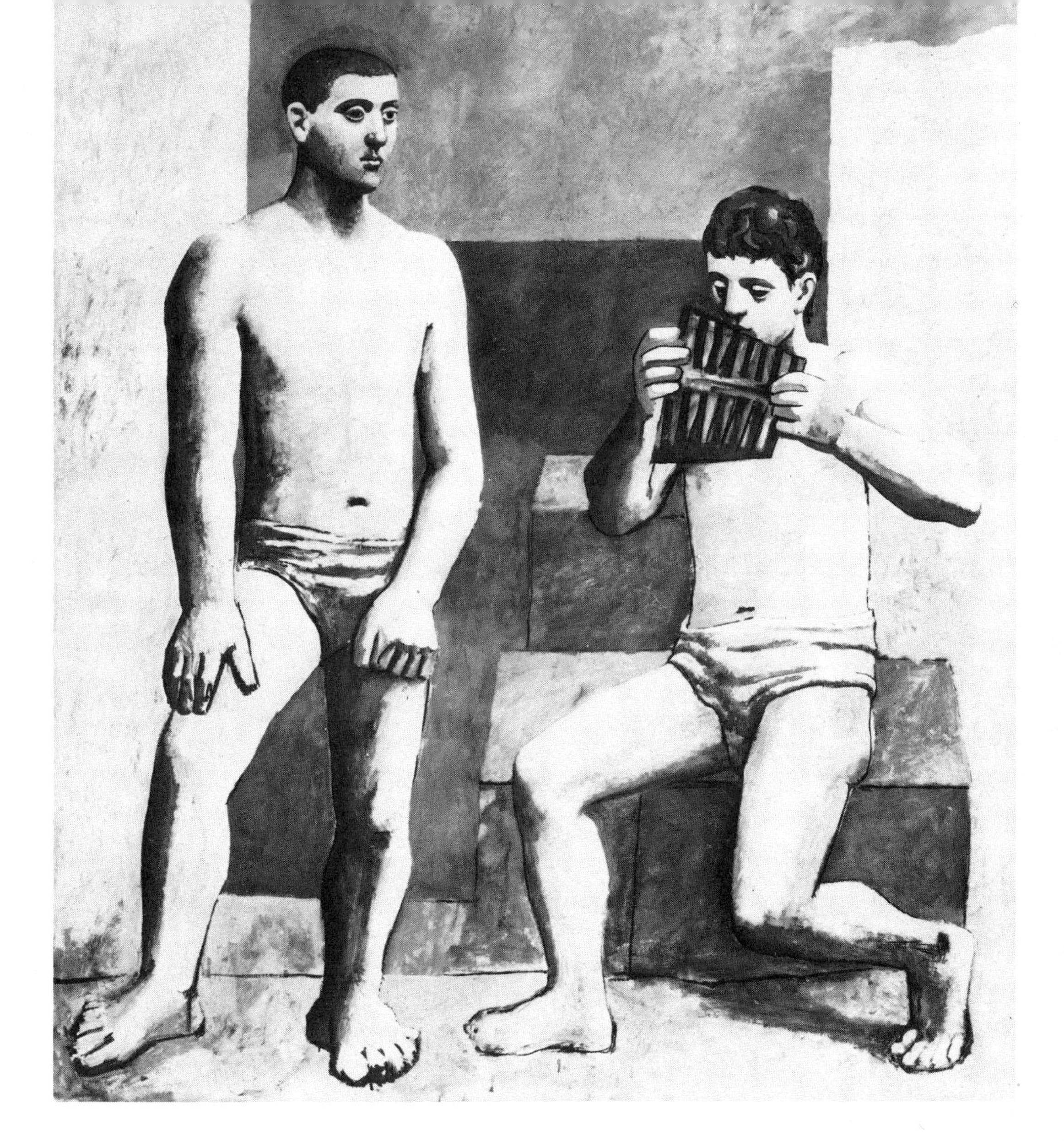

PIPES OF PAN — *1923*

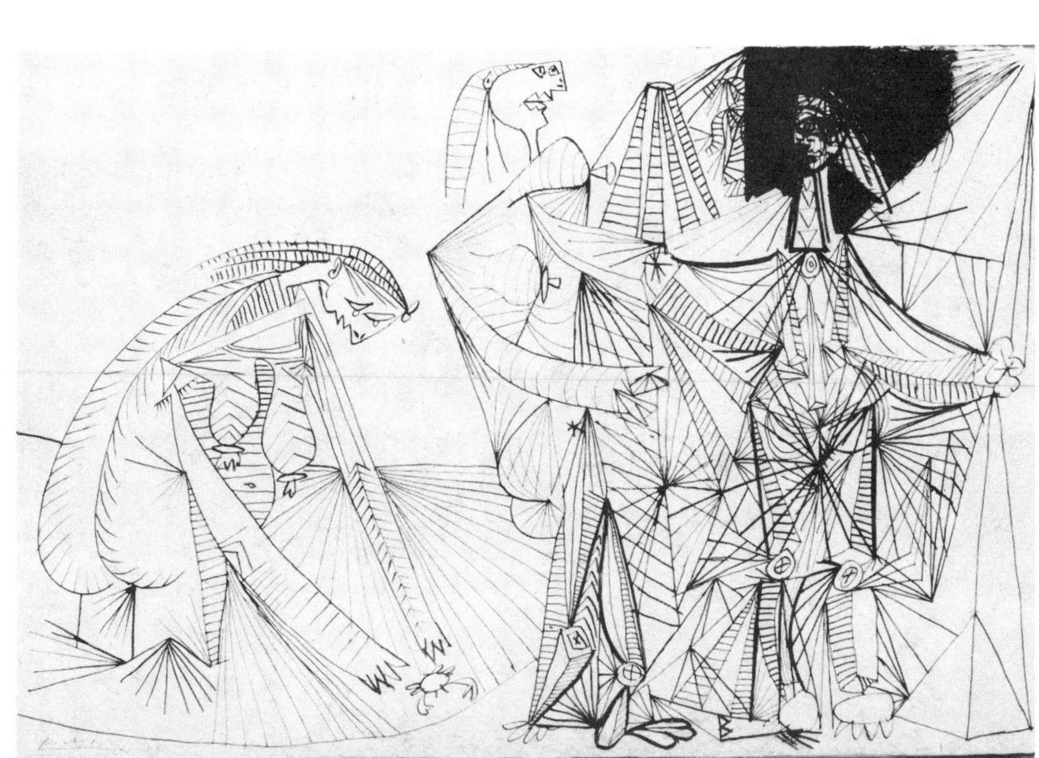

FEMMES SUR LA PLAGE — *1938*

THE SCULPTOR'S STUDIO
March 30, 1933

NUDE — *1919*

Of almost equal importance to Picasso's graphic analysis is his eye for allusion and association. When he has put together an image such as the bicycle saddle and the handlebars and shown us a *Bull's head*, 1943, we never again see either the bull or a bicycle with any certainty as to which came first. His mind is also stocked with the images of art history, and, like classical scholars in the literary field, he is inclined to quote, often aptly and wittily. In these circumstances his own remarks about 'finding' rather than 'seeking' are illuminating.*

Along with other old masters of the Modern Movement Picasso has accepted the public image of him as a hero. He has to some extent cultivated an image of himself as a whimsical revolutionary of an almost nineteenth-century kind; but the humour in his art does not reduce its integrity; for him humour is an essential element in all human aspiration. Every work that aspires to monumental seriousness comes close to self-parody if monumental is all it is trying to be. If it does not contain within itself some indication of human fallibility, some self-awareness of man's human proportions, then someone will come along and, quite rightly, put a moustache on it. Any significant form is open to parody and ridicule of this kind if it becomes a cliché. Picasso forestalls such ridicule by doing it himself better than his detractors could. He incorporates the possibility of his own fallibility, and then goes on to show us his serious intention. By so doing he joins the viewing public, of which, it must be remembered, he is an essential and an informed part himself.

---

*) Extract from a statement made by Picasso, in Spanish, to Marius de Zayas and approved by the artist before translation into English and its publication in *The Arts*, New York, May 1923, under the title 'Picasso Speaks':
'I can hardly understand the importance given to the word "research" in connection with modern painting. In my opinion to search means nothing in painting. To find, is the thing. Nobody is interested in following a man who, with his eyes fixed on the ground, spends his life looking for the pocket-book that fortune should put in his path. The one who finds something no matter what it might be, even if his intentions were not to search for it, at least arouses our curiosity, if not our admiration.'
(Barr, *Picasso, fifty years of his art*, page 270, Museum of Modern Art, New York)

NOTES ON THE PLATES

Plate I *Child holding a dove.* 1901. Oil on canvas. $28\frac{3}{4} \times 21\frac{1}{4}$ in. (73×54 cm.). London, Dowager Lady Aberconway.

In June 1901 the dealer Vollard exhibited seventy-five of the young Picasso's paintings at his shop in the rue Laffitte, a street that had become notable for the galleries presenting the most advanced art. Picasso shared the lesser position in the exhibition with a now forgotten Basque painter, who was twenty years older, named Hurrino. Though the public did not respond, Félicien Fagus, the critic for *La Gazette d'art*, wrote favourably: 'Picasso is a painter, absolutely and beautifully; his power of divining the substance of things should suffice to prove it.' Fagus also mentioned the various influences that were readily visible on the precocious surface of Picasso's work, but he also stressed what lay underneath, how soundly the artist had absorbed the traditions of Delacroix, Manet, Van Gogh, Toulouse-Lautrec and so on. He added a warning that the artist's 'juvenile impetuous spontaneity' itself contained a danger that might lead to a facile virtuosity. But this 'impetuous spontaneity' remains with Picasso to this day, supported by an equally instinctive sense of construction.

Children have always exerted a fascination on Picasso, but he invariably complements their obvious charm with a firm realisation in paint of the forms that he uses to convey their intense and direct appeal. He suppresses sentimentality.

This early painting combines several of the more reflective and entrancing aspects of art that recur during his life's work; the dressed-up child, the dove, and the ball which suggests a connection with the circus as much as with the nursery. The paint itself is robust and clearly outlines the figure. The density of the pigment replaces contour modelling and leaves the image firmly designed and related to the whole picture-plane in a manner characteristic of Van Gogh and Gauguin, both artists for whom Picasso had an obvious admiration.

Plate II *Nude: back view.* 1902. Oil. $18\frac{1}{8} \times 15\frac{1}{4}$ in. (46×38.5 cm.). Paris, Private Collection.
The blue tone that hovers in the shadows of the *Child holding a dove* extends its emotional overtones through many of Picasso's works of this period. In spite of a number of pictures, such as small brilliant pastels of the bull-ring, the colour so permeates his paintings that the name 'Blue' has been attached to the period as a whole. The colour can readily be associated with youthful, introvert romanticism but it is no less compelling or effective because it now seems a little excessive.

This painting is in fact rather less dramatised than the more obvious images of the beggars and mendicants that he painted. One of a number of pictures inspired by his studies in a women's hospital, the strain and the tension of this figure's back suggests a lean, hard existence. The head, buried in the arms, indicates a weary and screwed-up state of mind and body rather than a relaxed and dozing posture. A similar figure, from a slightly different angle, recurs in an allegorical painting called *Life*, of 1903, where it is seen as a womb-like image on a painting inside the picture and forming the centre-background of the composition.

Plate III *Family of Saltimbanques.* 1905. Oil. $84 \times 90\frac{5}{8}$ in. (213×231 cm.). Art Institute of Chicago, on extended loan from the Chester Dale Collection.
It is not surprising to discover in a young artist like Picasso, living and working in a foreign country, a response to and an imaginative identification with people whose lives apparently combine similar elements to his own. Actors, acrobats and travelling performers share with artists an intense awareness and purpose in physical action, which is contrasted with a drifting uncertainty of existence. They have a sense of timeless, traditional occupation and yet they express themselves in acts of glamour that are of momentary duration. Living from day to day, such people are aware of the inevitable ageing and decline of their basic aptitudes, which seem to face exhaustion almost before they have found fulfilment. Such a bitter-sweet situation must have appealed to the young Picasso, living himself with great difficulty but aware and nervous of his own enormous potential.

This picture is the largest of the works he had attempted at that time. The mood of the painting is one of reverie, the figures have averted, inward-gazing eyes, but the sombreness in the works of the previous years is lightened here by a pale and gentle colouring and by the day-freshened air of the landscape. The open, almost featureless lowland country, without aching mountains or devious crevices, seems to set the figures afloat, between acts, like a tide on the turn ungrounding boats and gently swinging them to a new direction.

The symbolism of the figures is general rather than specific, and they can be seen in several other of Picasso's pictures, singly and in groups. The identification of the artist with these people of classical and god-like ancestry is rounded out by his own profile, given to the tall figure on the left — the one person who seems to be dressed up. The character he has taken on, that of Harlequin, is of great significance to Picasso. He re-appears at intervals throughout his work, even visible as a presence under the complex forms of Cubism. Harlequin first arose, as a personification of the artist, somewhere early in the Blue period, possibly crystallised in the artist's imagination when he saw Cézanne's *Mardi Gras*, a painting of two clowns, in Vollard's gallery before it was taken to Russia by the collector Shchukine. So, interestingly, it was an isolated piece of imagery by Cézanne that had the first and more immediate effect on Picasso: the later great stylistic reformation of Cubism, that also owes something to Cézanne, did not take place for several years.

The image of Harlequin is more ambivalent in that it is indicated by a suit of clothes; the disguise may not fit, and thus the fact that the artist is 'acting' a role makes its effect more strange, and the viewer is unsure how closely the identification can be taken.

Plate IV

The acrobat and the ball. 1905. Oil on canvas. 58⅛ ×38¼ in. (147 ×97.5 cm.). Pushkin Museum, Moscow.

This picture is related in mood to the previous illustration though it is simpler in its dramatic intention. The little girl with slender arms and fingers, using them like delicate wings to keep balanced on the ball, is of the same type and inspiration as the girl with the basket seen in back view in the *Saltimbanques*. The young man, square and thickset, is massive in build; his musculature has grown with the demands made upon it. In a gouache painting, *The athlete* (Private Collection, Paris), the same figure is standing massively, legs astride, raising the girl above his head with one hand, his other arm not even on his hip to support the weight of the fragile creature. But his brute strength in both situations is refined and classical. His feet are still those of a tumbler or an acrobat; his head is more youthful than the divided cliff of his back, and the intense and fine line of his profile echoes Picasso's own features. He is like an elder brother called upon too early to bear other people's loads which have caused him to put away thoughts of his own aspirations. But they frequent his mind again when momentarily at rest in this in-between land. These pictures are flushed with a warmer tone of pink and the emotional content has grown richer. The circus people inhabit a more three-dimensional world than the figures of the Blue period. Life is still hard, suffering often acute, but achievement is also possible. These people are also artists, and, by expressing and acting out life for other people, they can find a purpose and a satisfaction in their own.

Plate V

Seated nude. 1906. Oil. 60¼ × 39½ in. (151 × 100 cm.). Collection Dr Vincenc Kramář. Picasso spent the summer of 1906 in Gosol, in the Pyrenees, after a brief visit to his family in Barcelona. The change to the warm rugged countryside undoubtedly relaxed and expanded his sense of physical well-being without in any way reducing his restless aesthetic curiosity. He produced many drawings and paintings; some were of the people and the landscape around him, particularly the women with their long straight noses and their heads made sculptural by being enclosed in scarves. He also painted several nudes in the warm ochre colours of the mountain soils. This picture, painted on his return to Paris, still holds recollections of the simple and monumental proportions of peasant physique and the associations of bodies of rude and vigorous health. But already the emphasis on volume in this painting has subdued the vivacity of his tourist eye to something much more conceptual and other-worldly. While the forms of this picture still draw on a rough vitality and energy, their sources are more complex and sophisticated, as much from museums as from life.

The figure is seated on a box, like that of the young man in Plate IV; she looks as if she has straightened up from a more elegant and classical post. The ground is earth-coloured and the background a washed-in lilac-blue that recalls an open sky but is more dense and close to the figure, as if it were a curtain. The body is modelled in two ways. First inwards from the edges of the incisively defined forms, like a drawing from the antique that is more concerned with establishing solidity than reproducing the illusion of the chance fall of light. Secondly, this slightly dramatised emphasis on the shadowed edges meets and runs over the broad, luminous and warm-toned wash of flesh colour that modulates outwards from the centre of the forms and flushes over the body, as if it were radiated from within. But it is the highly articulated features of the head that form the most striking and original invention of this figure. The inward and distant aloofness and poise that the head gives to the whole body does not spring from classicism, even of a heavy Roman kind. Its references are more to the Iberian sculpture that Picasso had seen in the Louvre, particularly some recently discovered carvings and bronzes that had been unearthed at Osuna, not far from Malaga.

Picasso was attracted by the unorthodox proportions of some of those heads and their expressionist exaggeration of the orifices. One can further see a resemblance between the sculptures and Picasso's paintings of heads in their oval shape, smooth foreheads, pointed chins, and by the heavily lidded eyes that are divided by the clear ridges of the eyebrows that in turn run into the long curved ridge of the nose. In the paintings of this period (Plates v—ix), and particularly in the drawings of 1907, there is an ambivalence about the triangular and pointed shape of the nose. In several of the sculptures referred to, the nose is broken off or worn away; what remains is a triangular shape that is made more evident by the curving incisions that run down on either side from the eyes to the sides of the mouth. In Picasso's drawings, and to some extent in the paintings, this suggestion of both plan and profile of a form being registered together prefigures one of the basic characteristics of Cubism — the simultaneity of views. In a more general sense, the proportions and character of this figure also prophesy the grand nudes of the early twenties.

Plate vi *Portrait of Gertrude Stein.* 1906. Oil. 36×32 in. (91×81 cm.). New York, Metropolitan Museum of Art.
See pp. 11 and 12, and note to Plate vii.

Plate vii *Self-portrait.* 1906. Oil. 35½×27½ in. (90×70 cm.). Philadelphia Museum of Art. While Picasso continues to make allusion to his own presence in some of his pictures, even now, this painting was followed by only one more direct self-portrait, in the next year. This is an extremely assured picture and shows the influence of Iberian sculpture, mentioned in the note to Plate v. But there was also the satisfaction that Picasso must have felt at his own first sculptures, which he made in 1905, and which had sharpened his desire to establish in painting a more precisely defined volume of form. This had gradually become evident in the figures of arcadian classicism that appear in the Rose and Terra-cotta periods. The fact that the sculpture he so admired had a somewhat primitive origin as well as a primitive vitality of expression also added to Picasso's desire to simplify the form of his work through the processes of the imagination, rather than through those of sophisticated illusion. He rarely worked directly from models. The head of the *Portrait of Gertrude Stein*, 1906, who actually sat for him a great number of times, did not satisfy him, so he obliterated it, saying: 'I can't see it any longer when I look.' He completed the picture only when he returned from Spain in the autumn of 1906, from memory.

This self-portrait is a remarkable design in itself. Parts of the image make reference to the sources mentioned, but it has a fine overall sense of unity. The palette, continuing the line of his trousers, recalls the self-portraits of Cézanne, as do the varying degrees of solidity by which the forms are expressed: a shoulder flattened against the background, as against a wall, or peeled away into the three-dimensional tube of the forearm.

The figure is to some extent still lit from one side, as in a conventional picture, though inconsistently, as if it were an object being turned in the hand. Again, depth and density of form is suggested by the asymmetrical drawing of the neck of his singlet which pulls the figure round out of the apparently flat straight-on view of the shoulders.

The slightly distorted relationship of the eyes to one another recalls that similar adjustment, found in classical portraiture, where, one eye being a little higher than the other, the viewer reads them as an entrance and exit to the volume of the skull. He feels the depth of form by being able to go in and out: so too, the slight displacement of the ear in order to bring it into prominence as a significant orifice, a shell-like feature, that not only collects impressions from a sensual world, but also makes the pivot and axis of the skull.

Over these efforts to solidify and articulate the form of the head run extremely fluid, curving linear strokes and lines that have an expressive of their own, a feature of Picasso's style that recurs in the heavy black outline of nudes, portraits and still lifes of the thirties and forties (see Plate XXXV).

Plate VIII *Les Demoiselles d'Avignon*. 1906—7. Oil. 96 × 92 in. (244 × 234 cm.). New York, Museum of Modern Art.

The precise significance of this work for our century is difficult to judge in so far as that for long periods it was not known outside a small circle of artists and acquaintances of Picasso. To some extent therefore its reputation was verbal and legendary almost before it was having a visual effect on other artists. It was not reproduced until 1925, in *La Revolution Surréaliste*, and not publicly shown until 1937. But for Picasso it was indisputably important.

The title, *Les Demoiselles d'Avignon*, was jokingly given to the picture at a later date by André Salmon, who suggested a resemblance between the subject and the ladies of easy virtue in a brothel in the Carré d'Avinyo (Avignon Street) in Barcelona. It is clear from the early studies and drawings for this picture that a scene of some allegorical kind was originally intended. One drawing shows a dark clothed figure of a man seated in the centre of the group, surrounded by the naked women and the fruit and flowers; another man, similarly dressed, enters from the left holding a skull. These two figures have since been referred to by Picasso as sailors. This adds significance to the ribald display and positions of the women and to the curtains that surround this intimate scene. As an allegory it may tend towards a parody of a classical incident, like the 'Judgment of Paris', or it may just as likely be an emulation of such a large and monumentally allusive work as Cézanne's late *Bathers*, which Picasso saw at the retrospective exhibition in 1907. Cézanne's late work certainly affected Picasso's style in a fundamental way. Then there was the example of Matisse's large painting, *Joie de vivre*, that also probably resolved Picasso to both extend and summarise his own growing potential in a major work. Picasso did not exhibit in the groups of his fellow artists so he tended to have less of the public recognition that went with the exciting events and journalistic disturbances of the Salon des Refusés and so on. This instinct for holding himself aloof underlines the preeminence of this work as a private statement of public significance.

As it worked out, any specific allegory that Picasso had in mind, evaporates, and we are left with a work that represents, without entirely explaining itself, the most profound development of art at that time — one man's assimilation of his influences and his emergence as a unique personality. Even this disturbance to the unity of the picture by the two Negro-influenced heads, added (so Picasso remembers) sometime after the rest, itself characterises his constant desire and his ability to keep on the move, to spring into violent motion just at the moment that stability is about to be achieved. Even with those bizarre heads, the total effect of the picture is not unlike the grand modulations and harmonies one discovers in a tapestry. The surface of the painting is not worked on for its own sake but it is nevertheless sensuous. Picasso's paint is rarely as deliberately 'painterly' as that of many other artists, of Braque or Matisse or Derain, but again, as the retrospective exhibition showed, Picasso is consistently responsive to his media, even when he is being deliberately provocative in his choice and use of material.

The significance of this painting then can be looked for and partly discovered in a number of sources. Some are private to the artist: his choice of subject, the nude bathing or displaying itself; his special interest in Iberian sculpture and the rude monumentality of Romanesque art; his contrasting response to the attenuated and expressionist forms of El Greco's painting, an influence that may be discerned in the astringent pinks and blues and the somewhat rock-like definition of the draperies.

Then there were, in 1906, the interests of an aesthetic kind that he did share with other artists. There was a general interest in assimilating both the forms and the vitality of cultures that were not European in origin. For most other artists, particularly those of the previous generation of Post-Impressionists, an influence such as Japanese or Persian or from the South Seas, was more a question of an exotic flavour, a romantic and somewhat sophisticated search for gorgeous simplicity. Picasso was much more concerned with purpose than with style, he wanted his art to be alive not historical. That is what Picasso found so impressive in the work of the Douanier Rousseau, a modern artist working with a convincing primitive simplicity.

The *Demoiselles* is a work wherein Picasso marked down a progression from his youthful, dramatised confusions towards a higher, more formal and potentially more dramatic form of expression. In the next few years this resulted in the formulation of the most significant aesthetic language to date, that of Cubism. It was a language that could be shared, as indeed it was, with other artists of genius but of different temperament. Cubism is not the only language of our century, but it was the first to be formed in terms of life in the twentieth century

Plate IX *Woman with a fan.* 1908. Oil. 60×40 in. (152×103 cm.). Leningrad, Hermitage. There was a lengthy postscript to the *Demoiselles* comprising many works in which the barbaric element of the influence of Negro sculpture on Picasso was worked out in violent distortions and exotic colour. The colour was basically decorative and emotive and the movement and the distortion that the human figure was subjected to was in favour of low-relief effects of primitive strength.

Picasso's imagination was still activated by sculptural influences but, working as a painter, he used his brushes like a chisel in soft wood — long clean scoops of paint. He did not return to modelling as such until two years later. But already by the end of 1907 a monumental gravity began to take over in his style, and sombre monochromatic sculptural forms emerged on his canvases. There was still an animal voluptuousness in such works as Plate X and a certain hectic agitation of emotion but, in these, as in a painting like *Friendship*, of spring 1908, the forms are of such solidity that Alfred Barr's term 'proto-cubist' rather than 'Negro' seems more relevant.

Plate X *Nude in a forest.* 1908. Oil. 74×42¼ in. (188×107 cm.). Leningrad, Hermitage. See note to Plate IX.

Plate XI *The Reservoir, Horta.* 1909. Oil. 31¾×25½ in. (81×65 cm.). Paris, Private Collection. A change of style often occurs in Picasso's work when he changes his environment. The desire for some sort of change appears instinctive and often casual, but when it happens his perceptions and the awareness of his surroundings are so intense that the sensations of surprise and wonder in the new place are quickly translated into the outlook of his pictures.

In the summer of 1908 personal perturbations and worries made him seek the relief of the verdant French countryside between Hallatte and the river Oise, with little idea beforehand what he was going to find there. An earlier interest in landscape at Corunna and Horta de San Juan had not resulted in anything more than sketches. As soon as he was, inevitably, involved in the refreshing luxuriance of a green nature his palette began to take over the colour. With the same incision and interest in stating the palpable forms around him, rather than their woolly and atmospheric Impressionistic qualities, Picasso attempted to make his landscapes as tangible as if he were arranging them on a tray in his lap. He suffused them at the same time with a drenched green tone that imbued them with the embracing cavernous mystery of late summer. In eliminating all fussy, particular and unnecessary detail he painted landscape with the simplicity of a still life — but a Cézanne still life, where inverted perspective, a mobile viewpoint and a rigorous sense of construction gave the still life the ambiguous attributes of nature.

The same deliberate affirmation, that objects in a picture could be uniquely identifiable as to their solidity and their 'presence', was applied to a small number of calm but alert still lifes that he painted on his return to Paris. They evoke the very silent, self-sufficient still lifes of Zurbarán.

The next summer, that of 1909, Picasso returned to the remote countryside of the province of Tarragona which he had not visited for ten years. Coming to the warmly lit Spanish countryside with the expectant sympathy of an exile returning, but returning with a new pair of eyes, Picasso was at once explorer, conqueror and lover of the scene before him. The deep shadows and green resonances of the landscapes painted the previous year were here exchanged for a Mediterranean light and atmosphere. This not only sharpened the visible horizon of the pictures but expanded Picasso's own responses so that he seems to flight his eyes across the intervals and crevices of the landscape as lightly as a bird side-slipping between terraces. But such physical empathy to the view did not deter Picasso from rigorously analysing it, replacing the picturesque effects of chance with an understanding of the firmly constructed organism that makes a work of art. By inverting perspective where necessary, accentuating the crystal facets of the forms he selects, he slowly spins the scene in front of us until we can feel the core of the hill on which these buildings are mounted like armaments against nature.

Colour, recently excluded from the strict processes of aesthetic interrogation, is here brought back with an enhancing and defining role, reinforcing the changes of plane by warm and cool contrasts of tone.

Plate XII *Portrait of Uhde*. 1910. Oil. 30¾×22¾ in. (78×58 cm.). Collection Roland Penrose.

The phrase 'the landscape of the face' has often been used as a poetic metaphor suggesting the sensations with which one searches the features of a familiar or strange but constantly surprising and expressive human being. If the phrase has become a banal figure of speech, because one may look just as superficially at a person as at a place, it regains aptness in front of a Cubist picture.

Even when Cubist pictures are most abstracted there is an intimate detail, a moustache, a watch chain, a hand, a curl of hair or maybe a piece of lettering — like your half of a theatre ticket — which enables you to establish contact with a new reality that will grow on you as you contemplate it. Coming from the landscape of 1910 to this portrait one carries over a sense of logical inevitability and appropriateness. The first demand commonly made of a portrait is met. Mr Roland Penrose records: 'So true is the likeness that more than twenty-five years later, although I had never met Monsieur Uhde in my life, but knowing the picture well, I was able suddenly to recognise him sitting by chance in a crowded café.'*

The painting is an example of the phase known as Analytical Cubism for, in spite of the identifiable presence, besides that of the sitter, of mantelpiece, books and the leaning backs of canvases, there is an overall disregard of natural appearances and a clear attempt to arrive at a maximum satisfaction of the senses by a minimum reliance on naturalistic illusion. There is a certain austerity of content which may match the character of the sitter. But it is not a puritan austerity, every plane of gradated tone is rich in implication and makes reference to its many possible functions in the picture, its position in space and on the surface of the canvas, its density or transparency and therefore the weight and volume of the form it helps to construct. Not least evident, in front of the original, is a delicate sensuous application of the paint that not only gives it a surprising human warmth but also adumbrates a gentle atmosphere that bathes and softens the crystalline analysis of the planes. Space revolves round the figure like time silently spinning about the axis of the sitter's thoughts.

Plate XIII *Nude*. 1910. Oil. 36¼×28¾ in. (92×73 cm.). London, Tate Gallery.

This fine nude is made very strict and elemental in its feeling in spite of the twisting, baroque pose and the cavernous, green-touched background from which the figure emerges like a grand tree-trunk. It is very still, as if frozen, but at the same time the accentuation of the long sharp-bent forms gives it a certain nervous and brittle tension.

---

* Roland Penrose, *Picasso, his life and work*, page 154, Gollancz, London

Plate XIV *Woman with a guitar at the piano*. 1911. Oil. $22\frac{1}{2} \times 16$ in. (57×40.5 cm). Collection Dr Vincenc Kramář.

One method of 'entry' into a Cubist picture, though not the most important, is, as I have suggested, through sleuthing the clearly visible realistic clues of detail. In this painting they are very tenuous, the clearest being the three fingers around the neck of the guitar towards the bottom of the picture, and the curving body of the guitar itself.

The simplest way in, if the style is still unfamiliar or difficult, is to take a point in the picture — in the centre and a little above the middle — and, by focusing on that area, allow yourself to become aware of the rest of the picture gradually, as a general mass; not by searching specifically but, as it were, holding on to the core (which is always there), and letting the significant parts gradually assert themselves. The presence of the figure, like the character of Uhde, is something to be apprehended instinctively. Of course, one searches as well, but it is the constant contact with the inner-felt structure of the form that enables one to build on that form with the exciting discoveries of the revisited parts of the picture.

The nature of the search that the artist carries out in a Cubist picture results in what is now commonly known as 'simultaneity' of views or parts: that is several significant aspects of any part of the figure or form are brought together in juxtaposition in such a manner as to reinforce the real descriptive power of the whole image. One aspect of a person or object that we know is added to other characteristics seen from other views. It is in the manner of putting together, of course, that the art lies. This application of distortion in order to describe more fully and accurately a figure has been known and used in art for many centuries, most obviously and symbolically in Egyptian art, but more subtly and less easily recognised (because familiar?), by all the great portraitists since the Renaissance. Picasso found the need to develop this into a total formal language and, with artists like Braque, forged a way of doing it.

Plate XV *Woman with a guitar (Ma Jolie)*. 1911–12. Oil. $39\frac{3}{8} \times 25\frac{3}{4}$ in. (100×65.5 cm.). New York, Museum of Modern Art.

While in one sense Cubism concentrated the character of an object or body, by bringing several aspects together that would not normally be seen at one time, there was a tendency for the facets or small planes round the edges of the picture to spread, to fade away, leaving the more intense core of structure in the centre. The actual space allowed for the object to exist in, even in a landscape, was severely restricted. Partly this was to inhibit the viewer's eye from swinging away romantically over evocative but illusionist horizons, partly so that the picture-plane itself be constantly remembered and the picture should exist as an object in its own right, an equivalent to reality. It was not to be viewed as just a reflection of nature as through a window. The oval shape of some Cubist pictures is likely to have arisen partly from the artist having no need of corners of a frame by which to establish the perspective in his picture. Perhaps also he had nothing very significant to put in them.

The paintings of 1911—12 show an inclination to expand and flatten the planes of form still further so that the whole of the picture surface becomes equally involved in the pictorial tensions. As these Hermetic Cubist pictures became more and more abstracted from quick recognition of their literal content, rather more active and positive clues of reality were included in the format. Such things as the lettering 'Ma Jolie' (a popular song of the day) or newspaper type became frequent. Nevertheless, the subject-matter of Cubist painting and the styles which grew out of it was always of sentimental concern to the artist. The subjects were, after all, the friends, the lovers, the familiar objects of personal and everyday environment of the artist.

Plate XVI *Absinthe and cards*. 1912. Oil. $13\frac{3}{4} \times 10\frac{5}{8}$ in. (35×27 cm.). Collection Dr Vincenc Kramář.
However much they tried to suppress the more opulent qualities of oil paint in their Cubist pictures, both Picasso and Braque rarely left a picture without some instinctive traces of surface sensibility. Apart from the landscapes of 1909, colour had functioned more like an enhancing blush than a direct statement. In this still life however, colour is used a little more insistently, anticipating the emergence of the decorative aspects of *collage* and Synthetic Cubism.

Plate XVII *Still life with pipe*. 1914. Charcoal and *collage*. $11 \times 13\frac{3}{4}$ in. (28×35 cm.). Collection Dr Vincenc Kramář.
In artistic revolutions, what causes other artists or the public to feel outraged is not always the most important or significant manifestation of the revolution. The rigour and asceticism of Analytical Cubism were hardly noticed at first as against the supposed violence of the assault on the human figure. At any time in history a fresh distortion of the body is likely to be read as deformity, as an insult to human dignity; any shuffling of the parts is taken as dislike or incompetence on the part of the artist.

It must be admitted that to a certain extent *collage* did begin as a piece of visual aggression. The artist, having already discarded or suppressed the illusionistic potentialities of oil paint, and yet desiring to make a work of striking reality, struck a double blow at the viewer who persisted in looking at everything in a traditional manner. The artist not only wished to touch the mind through the eye but to touch the eye through the mind.

The viewer would say, when faced with a work that included *collage*, 'this is a piece of wood or paper, or whatever it was, and immediately he would be thinking about what he was looking at as well as feeling about it. He would be thinking because he wasn't used to associating the actual material with a representation of that material in a picture. Still less was he inclined to accept the magic practice whereby the whole body of an object is invoked by a portion torn from that body. Nor was he inclined to accept in a painting so clear a display of several different levels of reality brought together. In front of a classical portrait such a viewer might be prepared to suspend his disbelief that a Stuart monarch might be clothed in the armour of a Roman general and be standing in the pose of, and possibly express the virtues of, a Greek god. Symbolistic allusion and physical reality are acceptable if they have been together long enough. But it was more difficult to accept that a piece of newspaper could refer to real life at the same time that it represented the shape or form of a bottle or analysed its structure.

An attack on the age-old integrity of traditional techniques was only part of the purpose of *collage*. The feeling the public had, that it was being joked with, was not helped by the fact that *collage* reintroduced elements of lightness, gaiety and colour and that touch of irony which artists wished to include once more in a style of painting that was in danger of becoming a cerebral exercise.

Picasso had preferred to regard Cubism as a 'transition' rather than an enclosed and self-sufficient movement. Certainly Cubism has gone on influencing art forms at intervals ever since. It has been turned to time and time again as a source of inspiration, both a discipline and a method of speculation. So when Picasso and Braque first included facsimiles of commonplace material in their Cubist paintings, then began using the material itself, and then later painted facsimiles of the appearance of *collage* it was in one sense a logical progression: in another light it was a visual pun.

The remarks by Picasso about finding art in waste-paper baskets were merely directed towards disturbing the snobbish preconceptions as to what may be discovered beautiful.

The materials used in the pictures were always subordinated to the total pictorial image. The amount of *collage* used was not, in the first place, very large, or at any rate covered nothing like the whole surface of the picture. Nor was a piece left bare, like a label on a suitcase, but it was integrated with the other forms of the picture. Lines may have been drawn across it indicating its other shape, i. e. its non-flat shape, or a portion of it was hatched or shaded so that it took itself back into the shallow Cubist-concentrated space of the picture. The Cubist side of what is known as Synthetic Cubism never relinquished the desire to materialise into space, however surface-hugging its component parts might be.

Plate XVIII *Student with a pipe*. 1914. Oil and pasted paper. 28¾ × 23¼ in. (73 × 59 cm.). Paris, Private Collection.

As the analysis of the object became more relaxed and the texture and variety of materials used became more freely applied, the pictorial image became more remote from a specific object and the metaphor of reality changed its character. Synthetic Cubism usually refers to works in which the balance is in favour of a newly discovered and more decorative imagery rather than the restrained objectivity of pure Cubism.

This gay picture is rich in tactile values, light-hearted in spirit, yet it nevertheless draws on the profound discoveries of Cubism with a masterful brevity and wit of expression.

Plate XIX *The violin*. 1914. Oil. 32 × 29½ in. (81 × 75 cm.). Paris, Musée Nationale d'Art Moderne.

The assimilated lessons and discoveries of Cubism are again, in this picture, spread with a light touch over a firm and elegant pictorial structure. The *collage* aspect of Synthetic Cubism is here imitated in the painting of pieces of material as though they had been cut out and stuck on. There is also an atmosphere of nostalgia about this recital of the symbolic elements from earlier pictures, the musical instrument, the glass, the lettering 'JOU' and 'BASS', the playing card and so on.

Plate XX *Guitarist*. 1916. Oil. 51 × 38 in. (129 × 96 cm.). Stockholm, National Museum.

In spite of the sanded texture of the paint and a rather sombre tone of colour, this guitarist still has something of the humorous impudence of Harlequin about him. The exchange of diamond patterning for a more formal latticework of spots, combined with the very tall proportions of the figure, give some hint of the 'sky-scraper' costumes that Picasso was to invent for the ballet *Parade*, the next year (see Plate XXI).

Plate XXI *Seated Pierrot*. 1918. Oil. 36½ × 28¾ in. (93 × 73 cm.). New York, Museum of Modern Art.

While Picasso continued to make pictures that face towards pure abstraction, he began again to make drawings, and a few paintings, which were representational in the conventional sense. Perhaps it was partly a compensation — for the perturbations of war and deaths and dangers of close friends must have sharpened his consciousness of death; perhaps it was instinctive to his nature not to place himself in an extreme position that would inhibit his freedom of choice, to do the opposite if he felt like it. Whatever disciplines he imposed on himself as regards colour, for example, he would never deny that a colourful picture was a possibility.

As far opposed to academism as he could be in the works of 1912 onwards, the series of drawings that he began in 1915 were marked by a purity of line and an assurance which have caused him to be likened to Ingres.

In the spring of 1917, through the enthusiasm of Cocteau, Picasso agreed, against his normal inclination not to travel, to go to Rome to work with Diaghilev on the ballet called *Parade*. The visit was brief — a month — but successful, and it was a prelude to the production of other notable décors. It was also significant in that it brought him into contact with theatre folk again, stirring in his mind the images of the Commedia del Arte. This time it was no longer with the mendicant overtones of the Saltimbanques family but the better-fed, energetic life of young dancers, belonging as they do to a world of extreme nervous and physical awareness, its rarified idealism tempered with athletic discipline — a world echoing the idealism of the Greeks.

Picasso was able to realise some of his ideas literally in the round on the stage, and also on a larger scale than he had been able to before. But this revived his acquaintance with the natural beauty of the human form in a way that no deliberate intention or number of hours in a life-class could.

Plate XXII *Still life on a chest of drawers*. 1919. Oil. $37\frac{7}{8} \times 39\frac{3}{8}$ in. (96×100 cm.). Artist's collection. This picture, like a number of other significant works which seem slightly out of place, has remained in the artist's possession for a long time.

Plate XXIII *Maternity*. 1921. Oil. Artist's Collection. See note to Plate XXIV.

Plate XXIV *Three women at a fountain*. 1921. Oil. 92×66 in. (233×167.5 cm.). New York, Museum of Modern Art.

Picasso looked to the spirit rather than the letter of classicism and continued to work in several styles, for no one style seemed adequate to express exclusively the flood of ideas which constantly rose within him. The birth of his son Paulo, in February 1921, obviously directed his feelings in the subsequent series of Mother and Child pictures, some extending the image of monumentality to the extent that paintings look like paintings of pieces of sculpture. In the same summer of 1921 he painted, amongst others, the two versions of the *Three Musicians* and the *Three women at the fountain.*

Plate XXV *Three musicians*. 1921. Oil. 82×90 in. (208×228 cm.). New York, Museum of Modern Art.

While this picture has already been referred to as the high point, the summarisation of Synthetic Cubism, it in no way prevented that form from continuing to answer the demands Picasso put on it afterwards, either in the lyrical aspect of his classical still lifes or the dramatic requirements of *Guernica*. In this version as against the more complex and agitated version (Philadelphia Museum of Art), the poetry and jollity of its figurative character are reinforced and set off by the severe disciplines of rectilinear design and the sombre richness of the setting and the masked shadiness of the musicians themselves. They are an alert but mystical trio; with their ambivalent macabre implications on the edge between *buffa* and drama they could well attend on Don Giovanni.

The three over-life-sized figures are seated at a table which in no way immobilises them, under which their companion dog lies – equally alert to their implications. Although spaciously composed, their environment is closely defined as a shallow box. Pierrot, Harlequin and Monk mime a silent performance that is activated by their minute hands.

Plate XXVI *Portrait of Paul*. 1923. Oil. $10\frac{3}{4} \times 8\frac{3}{4}$ in. (27.3×22.2 cm.). Artist's Collection.

One of the most intimate and direct of pictures; here Picasso's assurance of line is tough and tensile as a tightrope, one that he had to balance on over an abyss of sentimentality. It is this kind of achievement, the combining of the vulnerable delicacy and charm of a child's head with firm aesthetic statement, that should call for a phrase like 'magic realism'.

Plate XXVII *Cage of birds*. 1923. Oil. $78\frac{1}{4} \times 55\frac{1}{8}$ in. (199×140 cm.). New York, Private Collection. See note to Plate XXIX.

Plate XXVIII *Guitar and mandolin*, or *The open window*. 1924. Oil. $57\frac{3}{4} \times 80\frac{3}{4}$ in. (147×205 cm.). New York, Guggenheim Collection. See note to Plate XXIX.

Plate XXIX *Still life with antique head*. Oil. $38\frac{1}{4} \times 52$ in. (97×132 cm.). Paris, Musée Nationale d'Art Moderne.

This sequence of plates illustrates the wide range of feeling and mood that Picasso could draw from his immediate surroundings – from grave to gay – so that one thinks of the performances offered to Hamlet by his players: 'tragical-comical-historical-pastoral'. Cubism is used in them with a fluid mastery, particularly in the still lifes of 1924 and 1925; silhouette and shadow, form and colour interlock in free and assured invention.

Plate XXX *The three dancers*. 1925. Oil. $84\frac{5}{8} \times 56\frac{1}{4}$ in. (215×143 cm.). Artist's Collection.

This picture interrupts the great sequence of still lifes. No single source could be named to explain the outbreak of violence of which this is the terrifying expression. It is one of the few paintings by Picasso in which the actual quality of the paint seems to have gone through an unpleasant process.

It is disquieting as much for the authority with which it is designed as for the convulsive distortions of the naked, dancing women. There are few pictures that can be accurately described as containing 'angry' lines, but here the long edges of the forms collect and discharge their emotion with a shocking power, the sort of gestural release that ordinary people can only achieve by smashing a plate against a wall.

Plate XXXI *The milliner's workshop*. 1926. Oil. $68\frac{3}{4} \times 102\frac{3}{8}$ in. (175×261 cm.). Paris, Musée Nationale d'Art Moderne.

Nothing could illuminate the complexity of the creative impulse and the nature of Picasso more aptly than the juxtaposition of this picture with *The three dancers*. Although they share the sombre implications of a disturbed spirit, they represent or express this tone in very different ways. They are both large paintings of complex and interwoven forms; one is frenetic while the other is throbbing. The three dancers are creatures of the night; they are illuminated by raw bars of colour like flickering neon-lighting. As images they are wild creations of the imagination, they may break out and spread riot and disorder at any time. The milliners, though more complex in the construction of their physical existence in transparent and opaque shadows, are rooted in reality in so far as a milliner's workshop could be seen from Picasso's studio in the rue de la Boétie. They are creatures of daytime, immersed and confined in their box-like room, spied on through the window by the viewer's eye which penetrates with the grey daylight.

The picture is not without warmth of tone, the charcoal of the drawn lines is often picked up in the near whites and greys of the thinly applied paint — with little or no overpainting or secondary adjustment. The space in the room is felt into in a manner similar to the sensation of tucking one's feet under the table or chair. The curving lines are bent on constant motion but they do not set up a scaffolding of shock like those in *The three dancers*. Nor do they search or more than occasionally define a form.

They move one about the picture constantly but they pass over the function of establishing the existence of the figures to our apprehension of the picture as a whole. One is aware of the presence of figures in the picture, but their actual appearance and their literal activities can only be comprehended by submitting our responses to the irrational laws of a Surrealist-informed world.

Plate XXXII *Still life on a table*. 1931. Oil. 78 × 52 in. (198 × 132 cm.). Artist's Collection.
Neither the translated term 'still life', nor the graver and more impressive French 'nature morte', has been more sharply contradicted than by the glamorous activity of this painting. The sensual arabesques that may be found in pictures by Matisse of about the same period are here given an exaggerated sensuality which really gives them life. The corner of the room and the table itself, no less than the objects on it, are alerted into a writhing, hopping eroticism, a sardonic commentary on the passivity of human possessions — of the things we handle and treat as our own.

Plate XXXIII *Women and children on the beach*. 1932. $31\frac{7}{8} \times 39\frac{3}{8}$ in. (81 × 100 cm.). Artist's Collection.
Again a frenetic tone overlays and sharpens a work that relates, on the one hand, to the classicism of the beach, with its idealism and its dream images, and on the other hand to the disturbing forms those dreams may take. The emotions of springing, floating, swooning, swimming sleep, with a shock awakening, can describe or relate to both calming or ecstatic physical sensations.

Plate XXXIV *Woman in an armchair (Le Rêve)*. 1932. Oil. $52 \times 38\frac{3}{4}$ in. (132 × 98.5 cm.). New York, Private Collection.
This picture is more graceful, less extravagant in image and colour than the next illustration. Some traces of the beach goddesses of the early twenties remain discernible in the calm and simplified forms.

Plate XXXV *The mirror*. 1932. Oil. $51\frac{1}{4} \times 38\frac{1}{4}$ in. (131 × 97 cm.). Artist's Collection.
Similar features to those mentioned on previous Plates are found intensified in a large series of seated or sleeping women. Picasso rarely makes arbitrary cuts in the figure, in spite of the distortions he may employ. Here, he uses a classical convention of a mirror to add to the simultaneity of the views the spectator can see. It is possible to feel the whole figure embraced in sleep. But it is a sleep with undercurrents of uncertainty, convulsive in its depth; the rhythms of the wave-like lines of paint are not only body curves of outline but seem to rise and fall with breathing.

Plate XXXVI *Woman seated on the beach.* 1937. Oil. 52 × 64¾ in. (97 × 166 cm.). Artist's Collection. This painting is closely linked, visually, with drawings and paintings of 1930 that were constructed anatomies of rather bone-like segments, painted as if they were sculptures. The earlier figures were more open, space-penetrating structures, and they had a more aggressive Surrealist appearance. They were, however, like this one, set off against an open and serene sea and sky landscape. In this figure the greater volume in the forms to some extent subdues the external expression of tension or anxiety (Picasso must have already been contemplating his commission for the Spanish Pavilion that resulted in the creation of *Guernica* – see Introduction). The figure is folded on itself in a vast silence of contemplation, in this case of the feelings of her own body. It is one of Picasso's most powerful expressions of physical empathy; the face, which gives a monumental scale to the whole figure, is made tiny in its focussed attention on the entangled probings of fingers and toes; the elbow is an articulated but vulnerable joint; breasts and belly press ripely against one another; the back stretches and the buttocks open with the temporary strain of the pose.

There is a great deal made nowadays of the anthropomorphic shapes of sea-smoothed stones. Here is a figure, a sea-giantess, who seems to have inhabited the waves and shore for as long as any pebble.

Plate XXXVII *Woman weeping.* 1937. Oil. 23½ × 19¼ in. (60 × 48.9 cm.). Collection Roland Penrose. Returning to Paris at the end of the summer of 1937, Picasso added this striking painting to the various images associated with the creation of *Guernica.* In contrast to the other paintings, such as the *Horse's head* (Artist's Collection), which seems to be illuminated by an impersonal flash of electricity, this picture is more idiosyncratic. The features of Dora Maar are discernible behind the generalised image of a distraught woman who is caught unawares by some tragedy in her inappropriately frivolous street clothes. The robust and vivid colouring only seems to charge her convulsive grief with greater passion. Even the jocular stripes of wall-paper may plausibly suggest the touching emptiness of a nursery.

Many adjectives and metaphors have been called on to convey people's responses to this dramatic painting, compact as it is with visual metaphors of its own; 'grief biting', fingernails as frozen tears, and so on. Though it may give rise to such very pertinent expressions, it is a painting that strikes at the emotions by purely formal aesthetic means. By touching on the particular as well as the universal sensation of grief it makes its apprehension a common possibility for every individual spectator.

Plate XXXVIII *Still life with red bull's head.* 1938. Oil and ripolin paint. 38¾ × 52 in. (98.5 × 132 cm.). Paris, Louis Leiris Gallery.

Two similar still lifes were painted within a week of each other. Sabartés describes their coincidence with an acute and painful attack of sciatica with which Picasso was struck, and his extraordinary, almost miraculous cure by the cauterisation of a nerve. In this, the second version, the main image, the bull's head, appears both flayed and glowing with an internal human heat. The candle by contrast has the temerity of an evening star facing the setting sun. The lack of formal support given by the rest of the forms in the picture, which seem as if made of bent cardboard, isolates and perhaps justifies the identification of the images with personal feeling (the reccuring element of self-disguise), with the artist's immediate pain, rather than with generalised feelings, such as premonition of the Second World War.

Plate XXXIX *Woman dressing her hair.* 1940. Oil. 51¼ × 38⅛ in. (130 × 98 cm.). New York, Collection Mrs Bertram Smith.

This picture seems to me to be the extreme image of disquietude that Picasso has painted. The private aspect of the imagery in *Guernica* had, in that picture, been externalised and given to the world in a balance of feeling and expression; it expressed the emotions of others but the images had been wrought through Picasso's own empathetic passion. In this painting, Picasso, who was isolated on the Atlantic coast and intruded upon by the arrival of German troops, wedded together, on canvas, a monstrous image of love-hate, a mother-goddess with the feet of a fisherwoman. She is indifferent to the life her distended belly might hold, flaunting herself aloof in her private box. Hard, tough and ungracious, she yet arranges herself for an unimaginable confrontation. And yet this figure, like a female Minotaur, could be cast in the role of protective matriarchy, aroused and competent to defend her brood involved in their fatal games of war.

She is all the more terrifying for the utter conviction of her existence, her monumental construction. A child's rage, and often an adult's, is invariably destructive; constantly Picasso has turned his rage and his private frustration to constructive effect that we may apprehend with awe.

Plate XL *Portrait of the poet Jaime Sabartés.* 1939. Oil. 18⅜ × 10¼ in. (46.5 × 26 cm.). Paris, Private Collection.

The deprivations and discomforts of the onset of a war cause people to revalue personal relationships and treasure the company of old friends. Here Picasso ruminates on the face of Sabartés with whimsical affection, decorating him in a fancy dress of private allusion and gentle mockery. Like all fine and personal portraits (one can scarcely imagine Picasso working on a commissioned portrait), this one speaks of the character of the sitter with respect. It is a whole, good-humoured man that first strikes one rather than the extraordinarily complete exchange and re-arrangement of the features. The simultaneity of view is, in the event, no more disconcerting than looking directly at a person with a squint — one unfocusses and takes the head and the expression in at a general glance.

Plate XLI *Nude with musician (L'Aubade)*. 1942. Oil. 76¾ × 104¼ in. (195 × 265 cm.). Paris, Musée Nationale d'Art Moderne.

This is the largest painting Picasso executed during the War. The precise tone or attitude realised in this painting is difficult to define. One suspects irony. The nude on the couch, awake (sleepless?), is durable and tough in character, rather like the *Woman dressing her hair*. She is warm-coloured, sunburnt and fit, one could say. The blue, green and violet luminescence of the serenader glows as if it were a night song she had been singing — reminiscent of the brittle activities of *The three dancers*. But 'aubade' is a morning song, and the whole sombre tonality of the picture suggests the ruminations of people waiting for the day, hinting, with the stripes of the mattress and the arcadian guitar, of desires that remain dormant in the cool atmosphere.

Plate XLII *Still life with enamel pan*. 1945. Oil. 32¾ × 42 in. (83 × 106.5 cm.). Paris, Musée Nationale d'Art Moderne.

Picasso has at all times given the objects in his still lifes a symbolic character, partly by direct literal association, partly by fortifying the obvious shape of an object by giving it organic energies that can carry overtones. These may be contemplative, as in Cubism, or erotic, or, as in this case, even tragic.

Many of his still lifes painted during the war hold and express Picasso's most profound intuitions. These simple objects stand separately almost in ritualistic relationship to one another. The table top, of worn and wavy thickness, disturbs its own Cubist distortion. The warm grey background seems to hold shadow rather than light. Above all it is a silence that descends, the silence of a person contemplating more than what is immediately in sight.

Plate XLIII *Skull of a goat, bottle and candle*. 1952. Oil. 35 × 45⅝ in. (89 × 116 cm.). London, Tate Gallery. Just as a bull's skull dominated several sombre and monumental still lifes of 1942, and the lighted candle became a significant image in the still lifes of 1944 and 1945, so similarly the skull of a goat comes to occupy an important role in the paintings of 1950 and after. There is also a relation between the linear and fractured facets of form in this painting with the *Portrait of a painter after El Greco* (Plate XLV) and the large abstract picture *The Kitchen* of 1948. As with those pictures, there is here a suggestion of colouring rather than a direct statement, so that the complicated and articulated forms of the objects seem to change their appearance in the silvery, dazzling light.

Plate XLIV *Cock and knife*. 1947. Oil. $31\frac{7}{8} \times 39\frac{3}{8}$ in. (81×100 cm.). New York, Mr and Mrs Victor Ganz.

Again an image that recurs throughout many periods of Picasso's work, the cockerel. Here the content of the picture is combined with an assured economy of expression into an image of singular loneliness.

Plate XLV *Portrait of a painter, after El Greco*. 1950. Oil on wood. $40 \times 32\frac{1}{4}$ in. (101.5×82 cm.). Lucerne, Mlle Angela Rosengart.

The study and the subsequent 'possession' of a work of art by an artist can be as intense and valid as the contemplation of objects or of one's own face in the mirror. Picasso never merely descends to pastiche in these instances that occur time and time again throughout his work, any more than physical satisfaction would be the sole intention of one's affair with a lover-companion. In the deep sense, possession brings understanding of oneself through another's personality. The idealism of Picasso's character begins in the humility of admiration and continues in the respect of another's individuality. This is something which cannot be reproduced in a copy, but one may celebrate it by emulation and the conviction of one's own powers.

Both this picture and Plate XLVII are transcriptions that refresh our understanding of the originals. They even awaken us to virtues in those pictures that we have not perceived for ourselves, and yet they leave us with another sensation of living with a work of art rather than with the shadow of its reproduction.

Plate XLVI *Mother and child with orange*. 1951. Oil. $45\frac{1}{4} \times 34\frac{3}{4}$ in. (115×88 cm.). Artist's Collection.

Many paintings of this time are concerned with Picasso's young children, Claude and Paloma. Tender and affectionate, but without a sediment of sentimentality, they are the vigorous and colourful expressions of pleasure of an artist constantly and intimately rewarded by his appreciation of what is instinctively natural and beautiful. Parody and pun, the likeness between children and pets, and the optimistic uncertainties of children taking their first adventurous steps in the world are contained within a series of paintings that are painted with complete assurance in the complex shorthand of a life-time's experience of style.

Plate XLVII *Women of Algiers* (Final version). 1955. Oil. $44\frac{7}{8} \times 57\frac{1}{2}$ in. (114×146 cm.). Artist's Collection.

In the course of a few months — December 1954 to February 1955 — Picasso painted a series of fifteen pictures of which this is the last one. They are all free variations of a picture by Delacroix, called *Women of Algiers*, now in the Louvre.

Unlike the later sequence (1957), inspired by the Velasquez painting *Las Meninas*, where fifty-eight paintings follow the first and largest and most complete version, this series is much more like a set of musical variations. The theme is varied texturally and compositionally from one to the next, each having a self-contained quality, and the whole being rounded off by this jubilant and expressive coda.

Plate XLVIII *The studio*. 1955. Oil. Paris, Private Collection.

Again there are a number of paintings and drawings of the same subject but they appear to have no unifying dramatic point. This plate may be taken as an apt conclusion to our own sequence of illustrations, not by any means because it closes off Picasso's productive life, but because it symbolises the inner sanctum itself, that last, holy, but not, unfortunately, invulnerable place of private and mysterious creation. Here is a living workshop made comfortable by intimate and preferred objects, populated by works of art, pets, friends and family.

I

11

III

IV

Picasso

VI

Picasso
1906

VIII

X

XII

XIV

MA JOLIE

che

MANUFACTURES DE L'ETAT
50
ALLUMETTES FRANÇAISES
5c
CONTRIBUTIONS INDIRECTES

XVII

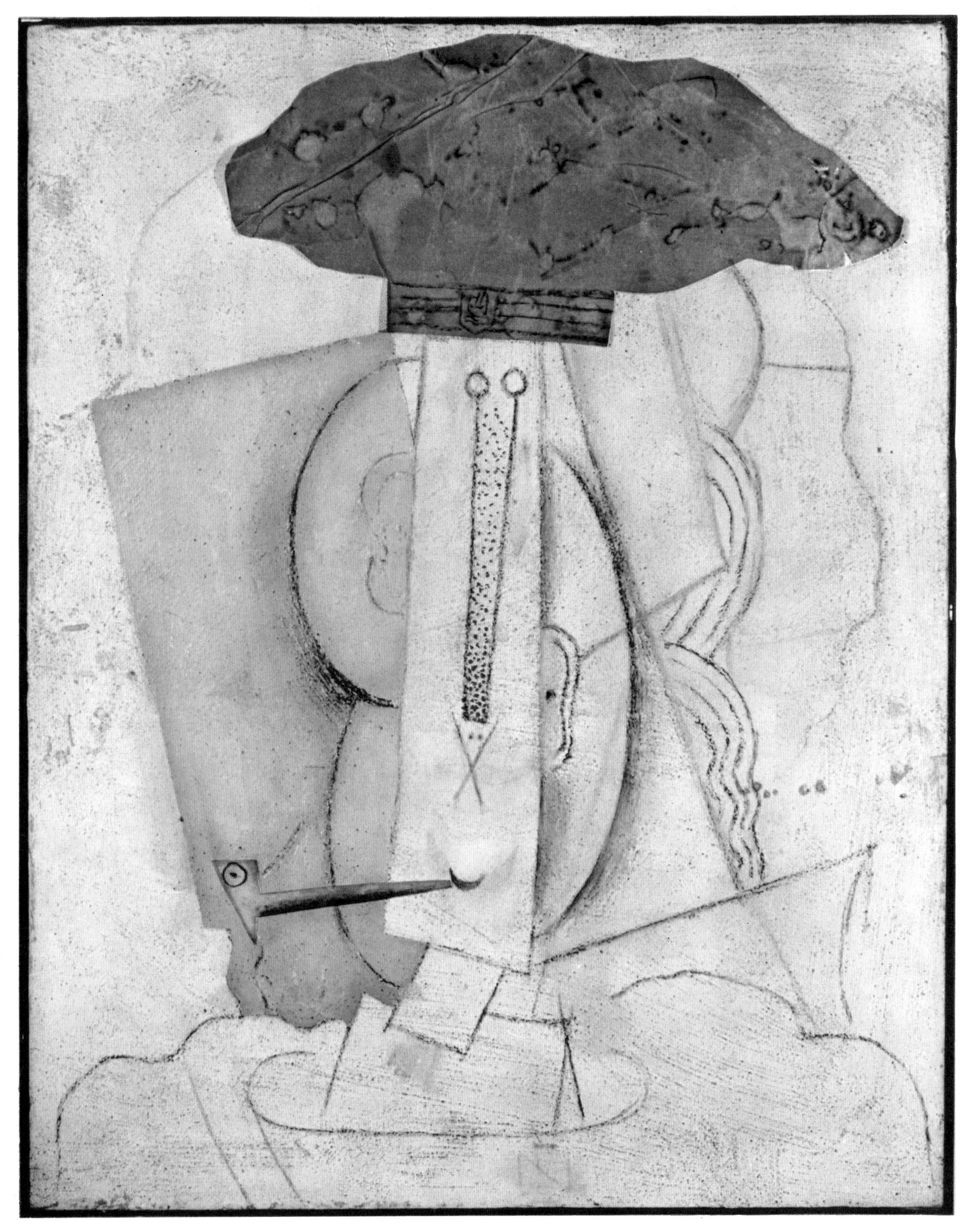

XVIII

BASS
JOU

XX

XXII

XXIV

XXV

XXVI

XXVIII

XXIX

XXX

XXXI

XXXII

XXXIII

XXXIV

XXXVI

XXXVIII

XL

XLI

XLII

XLIII

XLIV

XLV

XLVI

XLVII

XLVIII